Acti Learning Music

PIANO & KEYBOARD Book 1

Online video course on You tube

Acti Learning Music
Piano & Keyboard Book 1

Welcome to Acti learning Piano and Keyboard Method book. Designed for complete beginners learning piano or keyboard.

Learn how to play over 10 chords, improvise and compose in range of different keys. With online tutorials to give you the skills you need to play all your favourite music.

Our method includes: Improvising, Composing, Theory, Quizzes, Aural Activities andduets.

All tutorials and free resources are available on the Acti Learning You Tube channel.

Please scan the QR Code to access YouTube:

Please scan the QR Code to access the website:

ACTI-LEARNING

Music Made Magical

NOTE VALUES

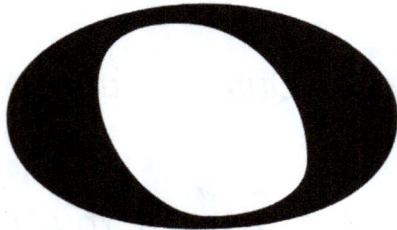 Semibreve | 4 beats

 Minim | 2 beats

 Crotchet | 1 beat

 Dotted Minim | 3 beats

Feel The Rhythm

$\quad \downarrow = 100$

Time Signature: This means 4 crotchet in a bar

Repeat Sign - Play Twice

Activity:

1. Tap the rhythm above.

2. Now try playing the rhythm on a C D E F G.

3. Now try playing along with a rhythm.

Black Key Improvisation

Improvisation- Making it up as you go along.

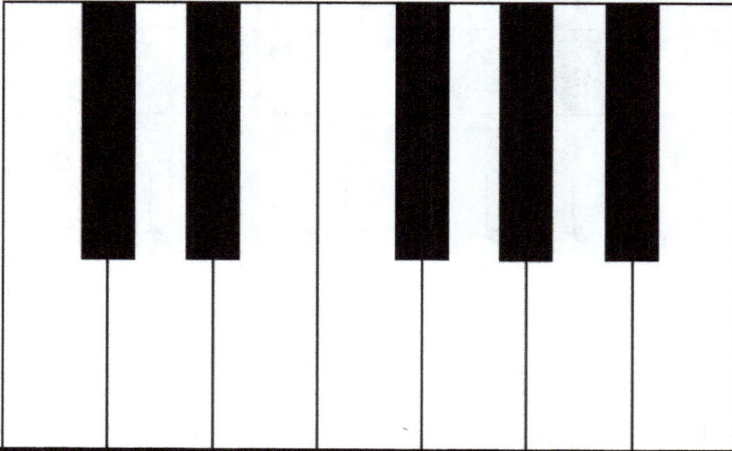

Activity: Use the black keys to make a song, and play with your teacher's accompaniment.

This is a music template- called a key, it can be used to make music, if you come out of key it will sound wrong.

Your teacher will start playing and when you're ready just play any black key.
Start with semibreves, then try minims and crotchets.

Teacher's part

Style: Latin/Mambo

♩=92

F♯   E♭m   C♯   E♭m   F♯   ACMP ON

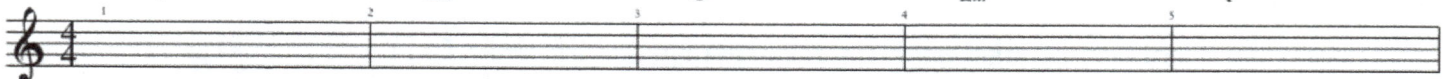

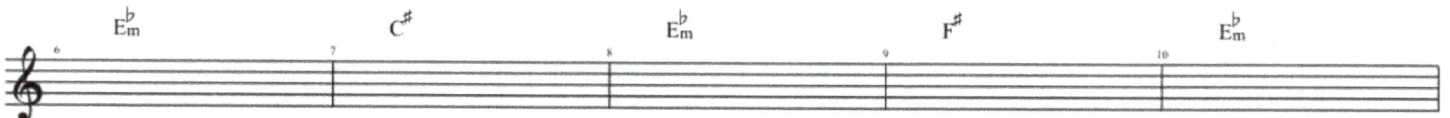

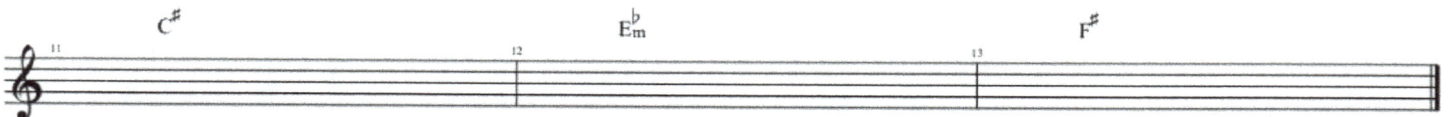

E♭m   C♯   E♭m   F♯   E♭m

C♯   E♭m   F♯

4

The Keyboard

LOW

HIGH

Play all the Cs from LOW to HIGH

Now play all the Ds from LOW to HIGH

Now play all the Es from LOW to HIGH

Now go from HIGH to LOW

Then try F G A B

The Stave & Basics

1. Music is written on a STAVE (staff) it has five lines.

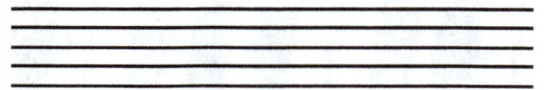

2. Notes are written on the LINES or in the SPACES.

3. Middle C is the centre of the keyboard. The notes higher than Middle C are written on the treble clef.

4. Middle C had it's own line below the STAVE.

The Keys

EACH NOTE ON THE STAVE
SHOWS ONE NOTE ON THE KEYBOARD

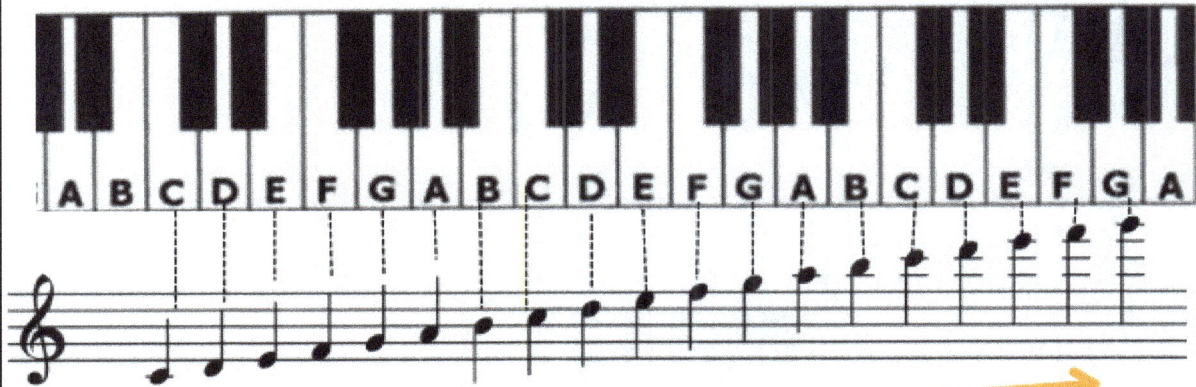

A B C D E F G A B C D E F G A B C D E F G A

The notes go up from line to space

EACH NOTE GETS GRADUALLY HIGHER

Try playing all the notes listed above. Say
them as you play them

Finger Numbers

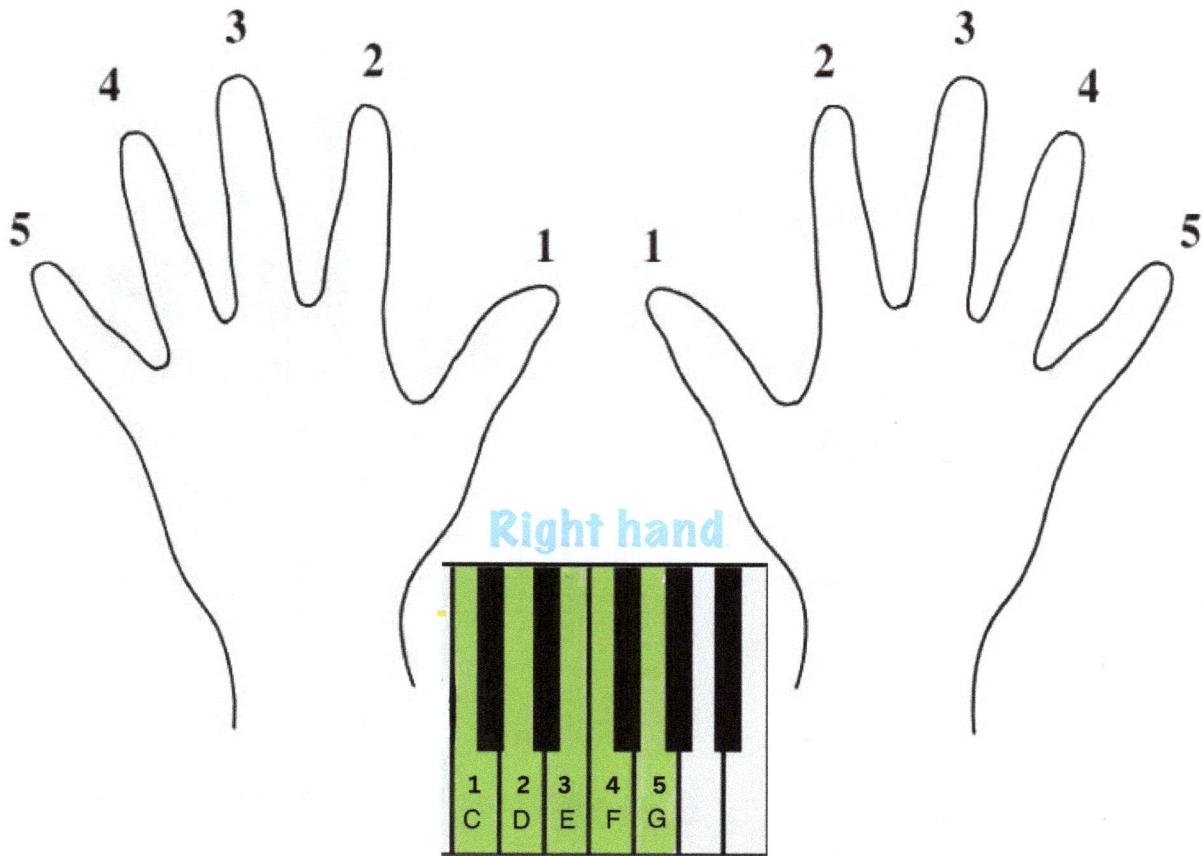

Right hand

1. Put your right hand thumb on C. One finger on each key. It should be:

C D E F G

Finger Numbers: 1 2 34 5

2. Now Play finger numbers to warm up:

111

222

3345

12345

54321

Exercises

Slow: ♩ =90bpm

Fast: ♩ =140bpm

Style: March

1. TRY THESE EXERCISES WITH YOUR RIGHT HAND

2. Now try and play along with the backing tracks

LEVEL 1 NOTES

Finger Numbers: **1**   **2**   **3**   **4**   **5**

C D E F G

This is a
C 5 Finger scale:

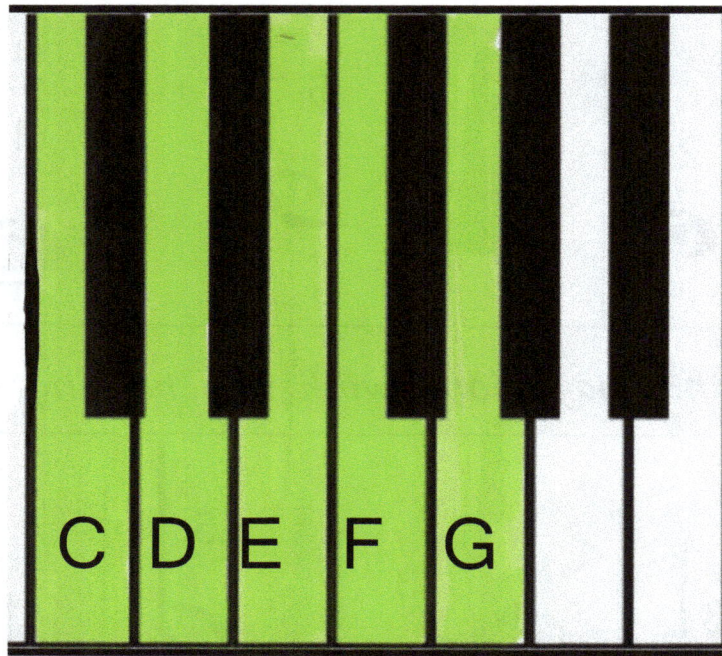

Write the note name under the stave.

10

C Rhythms

Style: Rnb Modern

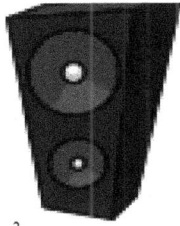

♩=100 - 140

Sweet Harmonies

Style: PopBallard

♩=100

C Rhythms Teacher Duet

♩=140 C   G   F   C   G   F   C   G   F G   C G   C

Sweet Harmonies Teacher Duet

♩=100 C   G   C   G   C

11

The Easy Tune

Style: Latin/Bossa
Voice: NylonGuitar

♩ = 100

I know how to play a tune   C   C   G   C   C   G

it is eas -y   watch and see   G   G   G   C   C   C

Easy Tune 2

Style and voice As above

♩ = 100

Minor Nocturne

Style: JazzWaltz
Voice: TenorSax

♩ = 100

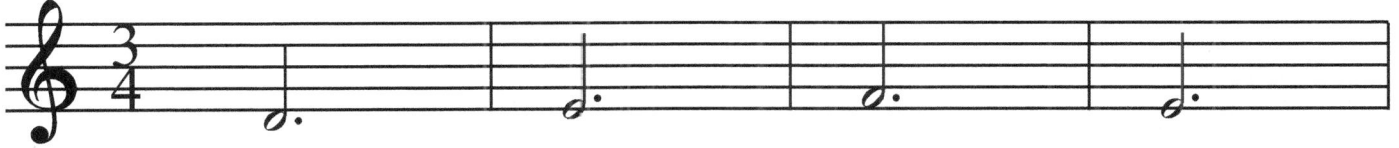

Try playing at a fastest tempo. Can you play up to 140BPM?

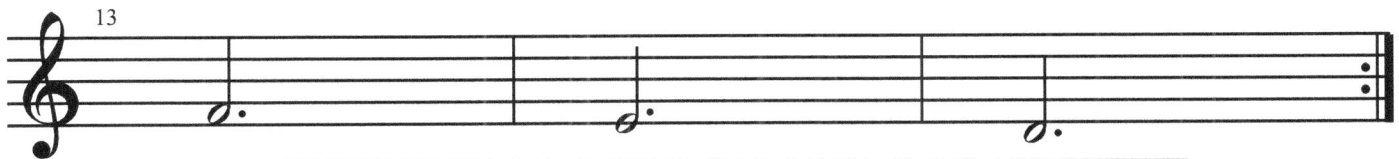

Nocturne- Romantic style music inspired by the night.

Teacher duet

ACMP ON

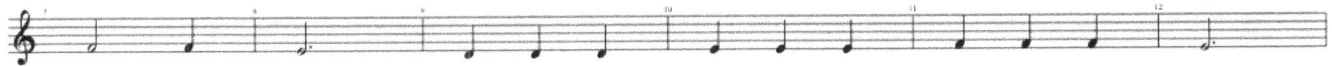

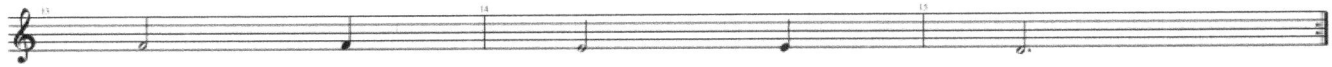

The Lazy-Eyed Lullaby

Style: Country

$\quad \downarrow = 100$

Teacher Duet

$\downarrow = 10$

Alouette

Voice: GrandPiano
Style: Ballard

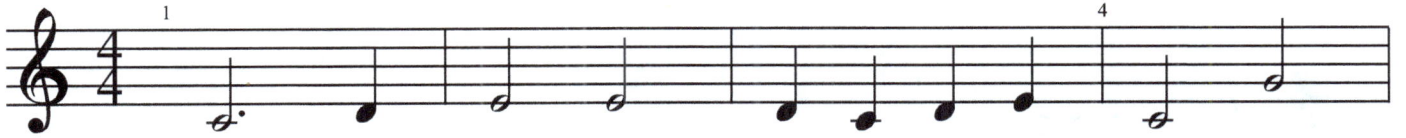

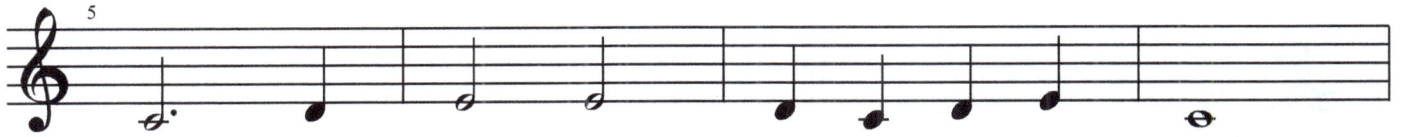

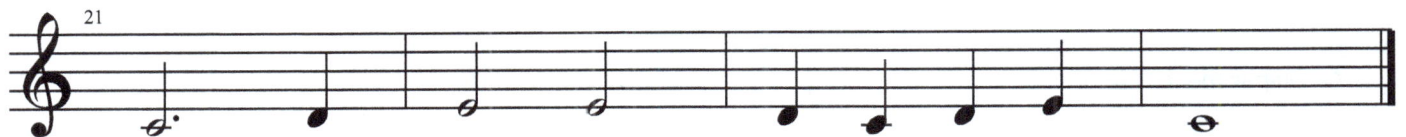

♩=100

Stepping

070 Foxtrot
018 Nylon Guitar

♩=125

Step- ping down to   C   C   step- ping down yes   you   and   me!

Line space line   space   line space line   space   up   and   down we   go.

Skipping

♩=85

I   am   skip- ping   on   the   keys   will you come and   watch me   please?

C   E   G   G   E   C   wont you   skip   with   me?

Accompaniment

ACMP ON

♩=100

C	G	F	G	C	G	F	G	C
1	2	3	4	5	6	7	8	9

16

Improvising in C

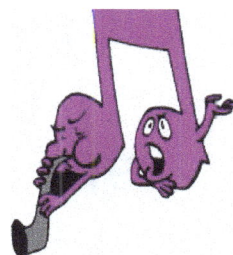

Let's try and improvise using the **C Major 5 Finger scale. Listen to the accompaniment and get a feel for the music. Then when you are ready start making up anything you like.** Make sure your song is on beat, If you struggle try sticking to minims.

If you play any black note, it won't sound great! Because it is out of **KEY.**
If you're brave try and play out of key to hear how it sounds.

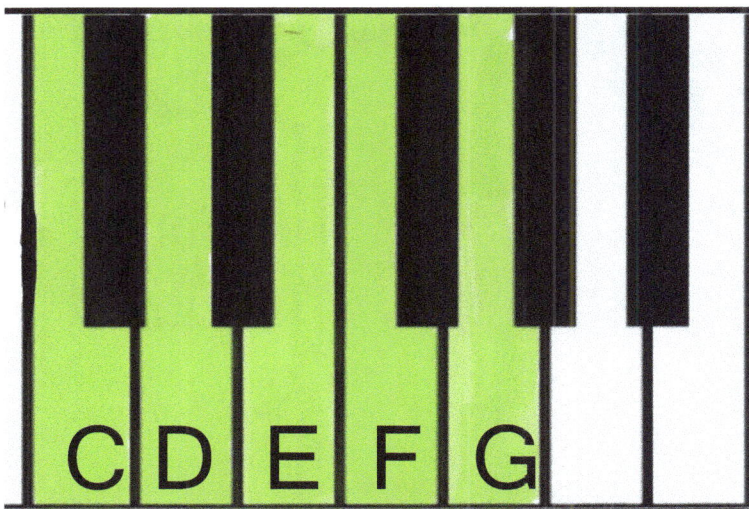

Style:_____

To finish
end to end on___

Improvisation Accompaniment

ACMP CN

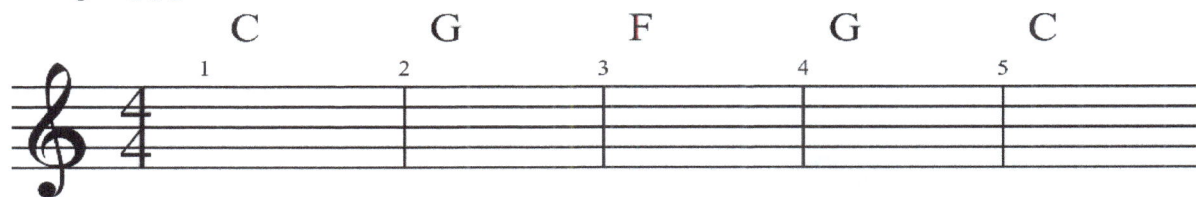

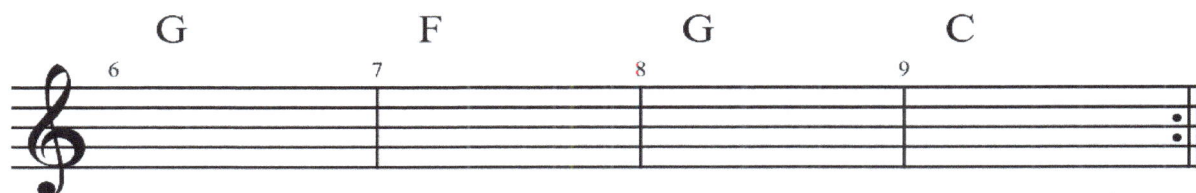

17

Dynamics!

Try these different Dynamics if your keyboard is touch sensitive.

Getting Louder

p < mf < f

Piano - Soft

Mezzo-forte - Moderately Loud

Forte - Loud

> Getting Softer

mp Mezzo-Piano - Moderately Soft

Dotted Minims

Style: JazzWaltz
Voice: Guitar

♩ =125

Teacher duet   *ACMP ON*

♩=125

| C | G | Em | G | C | G | Em | G |

| C | G | C | G | Em | C |

19

Grooving in C

Style: Rock & Roll
Voice: Flute
♩=150-180

1. How many Gs can you find in this music?

2. How many Ds can you find in this music?

3. How many Minims in this music?

4. Where does Section A begin and end?

Ode To Joy

Beethoven

♩=120   Style: Ballard
          Voice: Cello

Teacher Duet

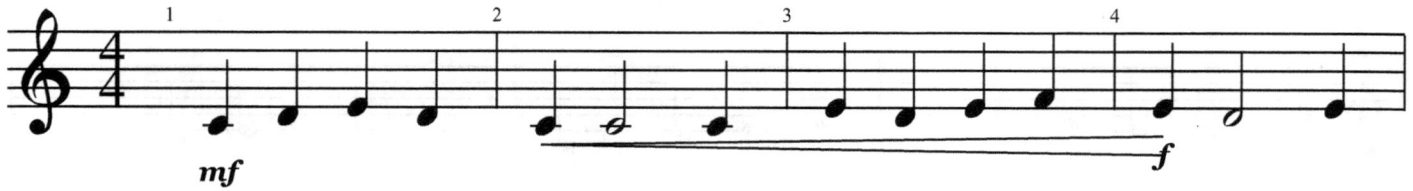

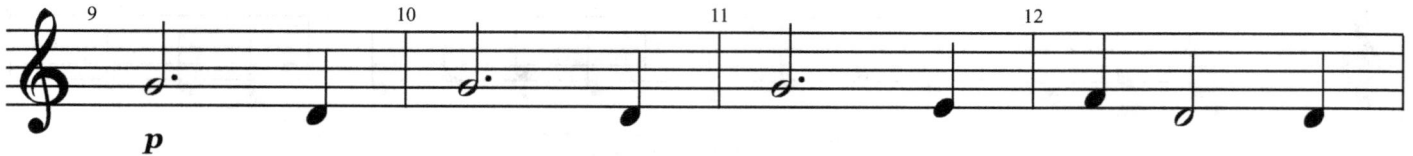

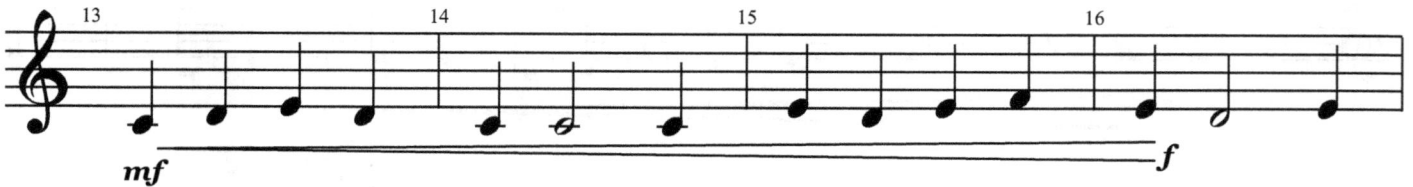

1. How many dotted minims are there?
2. How many crotchets?
3. There are 6 Crotchet Fs. True or False?
4. How many Cs are there?
5. How many beats are in each bar ?
6. What is the highest note?
7. Which bars play the notes G F E D?
8. How many times is the rhythm in Bar 2 played?
9. How many Fs are there in this music?
10. How many times is the rhythm in Bar 9 played?
11. Bar 1 - 8 is the A section. Where is section A played again. Highlight it on the music.

22

♩ = 100-150

Left hand Exercises

Style: Reel/March

23

♩ = 100 -130

Style:Dance

1. Fill in the missing Finger Numbers.

2. Try this exercises with a metronome and then a keyboard rhythm.

Chords

Chords are more than one note played at the same time. Some chords sound good and others don't. A harmonise chord is pleasant sounding.
Pleasantly harmonised chords are called MAJOR chords.

Aural Activity: Listen to your teacher play some chords, see if you can hear the harmonised chords.

There's a chord for each note: C major, D major, E major, F major, G major, A major and B major.

The C Major Chord

1st 2nd 3rd 4th 5th

A C Major chord is made of the 1st 3rd and 5th note of the C Major scale. This creates a perfectly harmonised chord.

Play the C chord

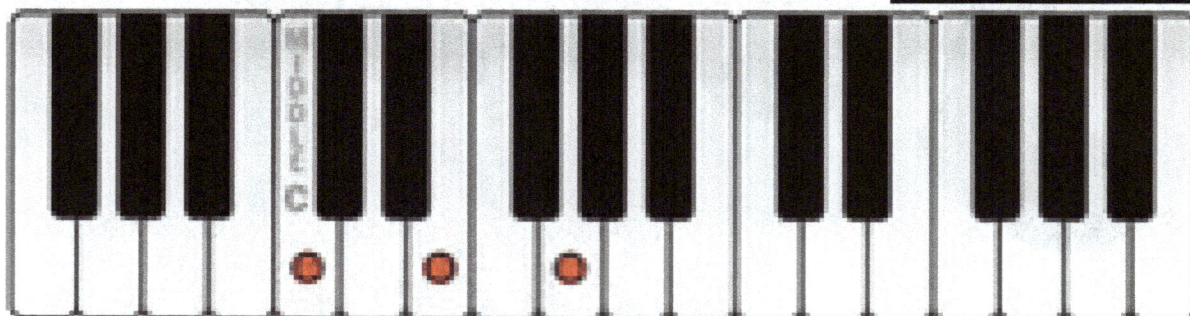

The Bell

Exercise 1

Style: PopBallard

♩=100

C | C | C | C
C | C | C | C

Exercise 2

C | C | C | C
C | C | C | C

27

Inverted
C MAJOR

The same chord- arranged in a different order.

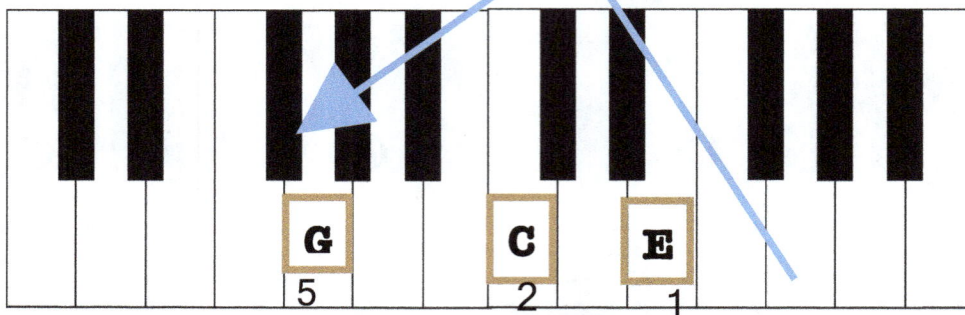

G
5

C
2

E
1

To make it easier to move to other chords - play the C major chord in a different way, it's called an inverted chord.

The same notes arranged differently- play the G with the 5th finger.

Try it - Play G - C E

Hold it for four beats and play along with your favourite Keyboard rhythm.

Rising Sun

Style: Swing

♩=100

Can you play this with the inverted C major chord ?

The G Major CHORD

G A B C D

1st 2nd 3rd 4th 5th

The G chord is made of the 1st 3rd and 5th note of the 5 finger scale.

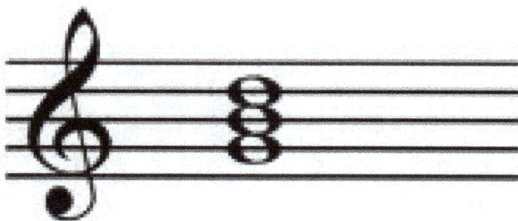

Practice moving from a C to a G chord.
It is easier if you use the inverted C chord

G B D

30

The Easy Tune With Chords

Style: Latin/Bossa
Voice: SlapBass

♩ = 130-150

ACMP ON

mp I know how to play a tune C C G C C G

it is eas -y watch and see G G G C C C

The Easy Tune 2 With Chords

Style and Voice as above

ACMP ON

♩ = 100

Alouette

Voice: Guitar
Style: 8Beat
♩=100

With chords

Abella

Style: SlowRock

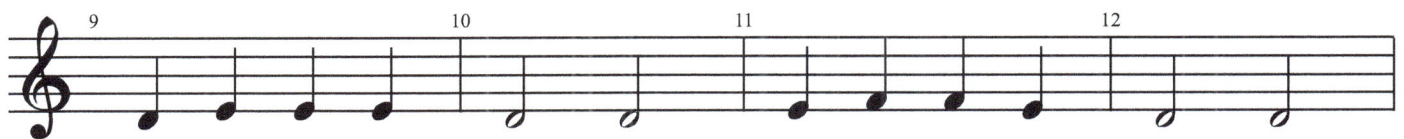

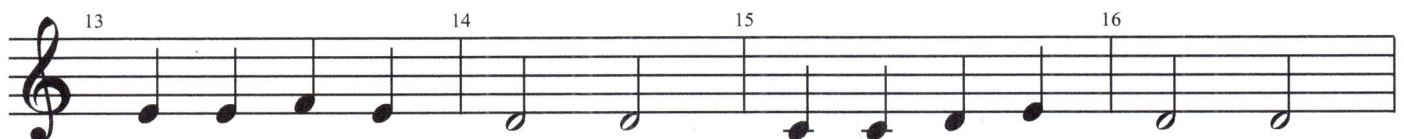

1. There are 49 Crotchets all together. True or false ?
2. How many Ds are there?
3. How many G chords are there?
4. How many beats in each bar?
5. There are 17 Es all together. True or False?
6. How many semibreve Ds are there?
7. How many times is bar 1 played?
8. How many times is Bar 3 played?

- 1 -

Mary Had A little Lamb

Style: _____

Voice: _____

Add the missing C or G chords to the empty boxes.

♩=100

1. Did you notice a relationship between the melody and the chords?

THE F MAJOR CHORD

Practice the following chord pattern:

C 1 2 3 4
G 1 2 3 4
F 1 2 3 4
G 1 2 3 4

Now try:
F 1 2 3 4
G 1 2 3 4
C 1 2 3 4
G 1 2 3 4

Calypso Chords

Try playing the chords pattern - Start slowly
and build up the tempo!

Style:Reggae

♩=88   C   F   G

1   2   3

C   F   G

4   5   6

C   F   G

7   8   9

C   C

10   11

Can you Improvise a melody to play with the chords? Play you melody as
minims.

36

C Harmonies

Voice: Guitar
Style: Rumba
♩ = 130

Q1. Highlight Section A
Q2. Does this piece have a ABA or AABB structure?

Study 1

Style: HipHop

ACMP OM

♩ = 80

Study 2

Style as above

ACMP ON

♩ = 145

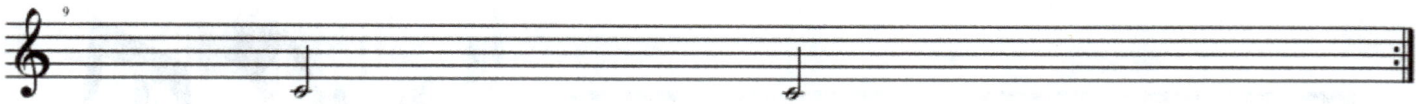

Andante Waltz

Style: Watlz/Musette

Can you add the remaining C G or F Chords to this melody

♩=100

Can you add your own dynamics?

Legato - Smoothly

Legato is the technique of smooth notes that have not break in sound, each note should feel connected to each other.

Legato is shown through the slur.

Staccato Chops

Style:Swing

♩=120

1. How many times in Bar 2 played?

2. How many Gs are there?

3. What is the tempo of this piece?

4. How many times in Bar 1 played?

5. How many times in the chord pattern; F C G C played?

The FACE Treble clef NOTES

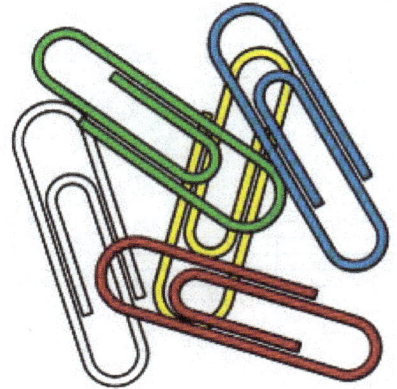

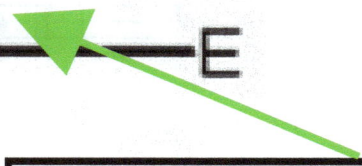

F
E
D
C
B
A
G
F
E

The notes in the spaces spell FACE

1. Can you match the notes with the correct names?

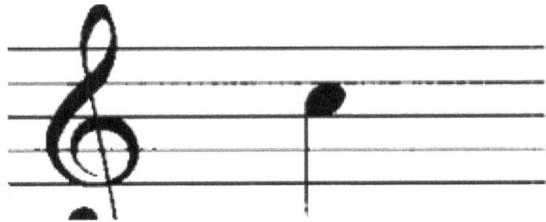

E

C

A

F

2. Can you write the note names?

BONUS QUESTION!

_____

44

The A minor 5 Finger Scale

| A | B | C | D | E |

1st 2nd 3rd 4th 5th

The A minor Chord | Am

A C E

45

A minor Steps and Skips

Voice: TenorSax
Style: Samba

ACMP ON

♩ = 120

Am — C — Am — C

Finger 1 on A

Am — C — Am — Am

A Minor Study

Style and Voice as above

ACMP ON

120

Am — C — F — G

F — G — Am — Am

Try to transpose the melody to D minor. Play the same pattern but start on D.

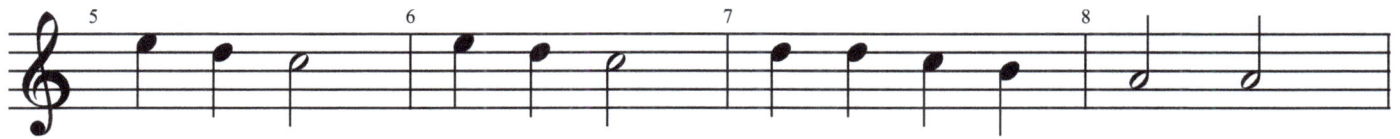

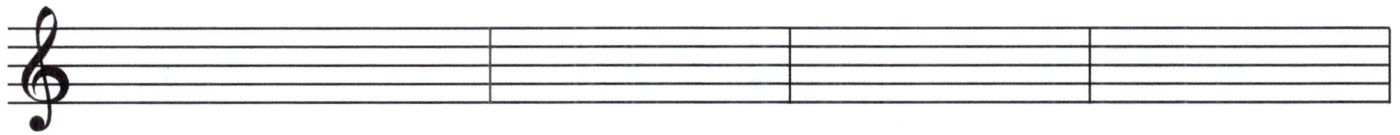

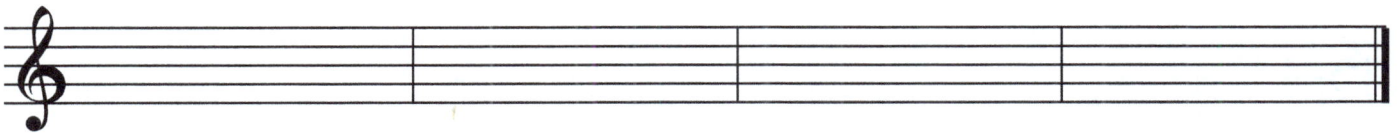

Sweet Lady

Voice: E.Piano
Styele: 16Beat

In C major

Improvise your own melody in C using the chords from Sweet lady.

Ties

When you see two of the same notes connected with a curved line it is called a tie. The two notes values are added together.

The minim plus crotchet = 3 beats

Due to the tie, you will add these values together.

This will be held for 2 beats

This will be 5 beats total

49

Bohemian Melody
in A Minor

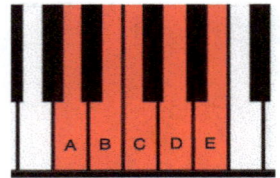

Style: Tango
Voice: Bass

1. Try and tap the rhythm before you play, to get use to the ties.

2. Can you Improvise your own melody in A Minor? Add your own Chords Am, G and F.

Lunar Eclipse

In A Minor

Voice: Flute
Style: Jazz Waltz

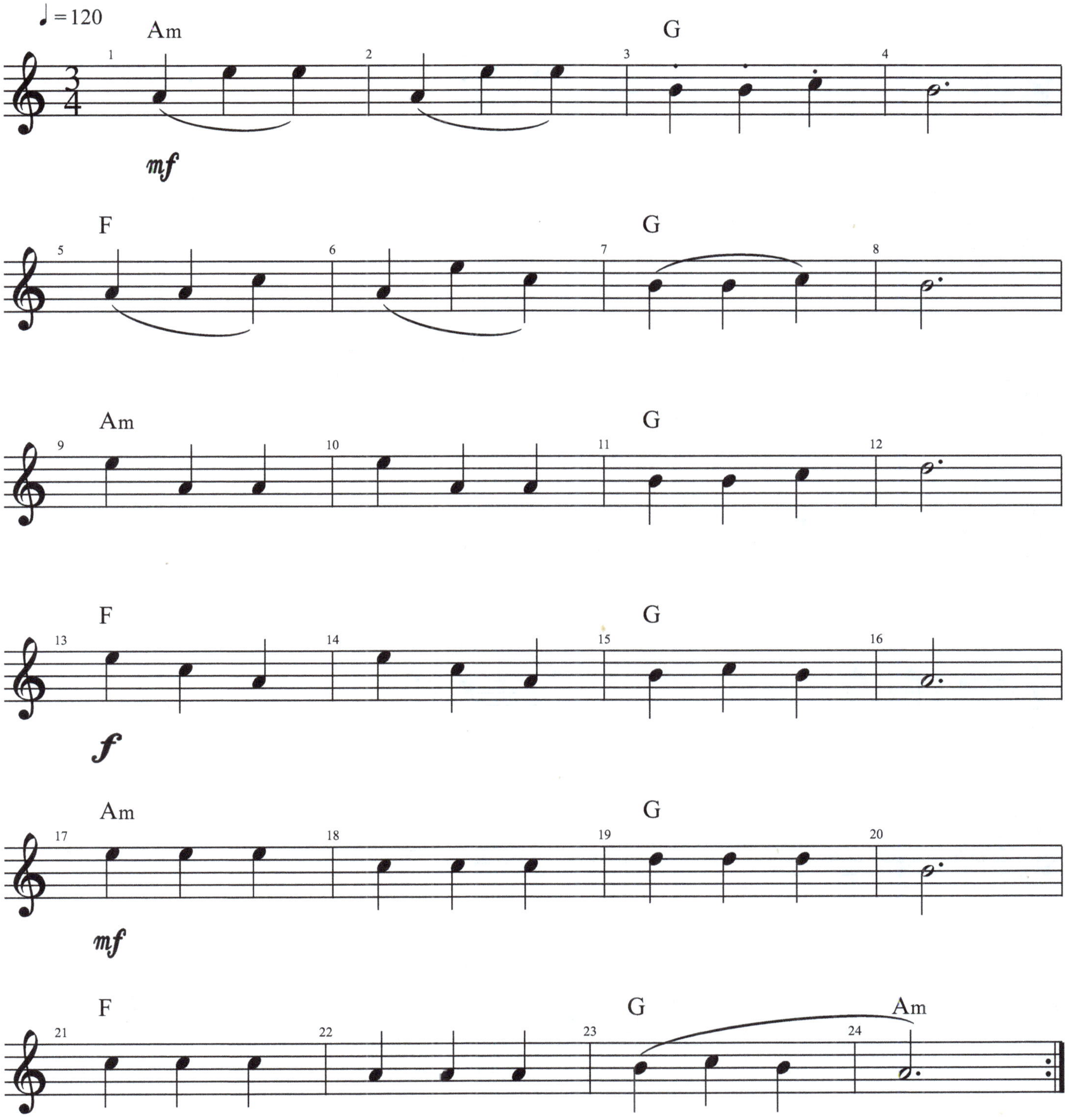

The Jazz Spot

The Treble C 5 finger scale:

New Chord - Em - E minor - See page 63

52

The C major scale

1. Write each note name above each note.

| 1 | 2 | 3 | (1) | 2 | 3 | 4 | 5 | 4 | 3 | 2 | 1 | (3) | 2 | 1 |

Tuck your thumb under

Third finger over thumb

The C major scale is like a ladder showing all notes in the key of C major. The function of the scale will become clearer the more you progress. For now you should try and learn to play this scale from memory with the correct finger pattern.

2. Can you write the finger numbers under each note?

3. Circle the finger changes.

Unit 8

Sharps

Half a step/ Semitone

C#	D#	F#	G#	A#	C#	D#

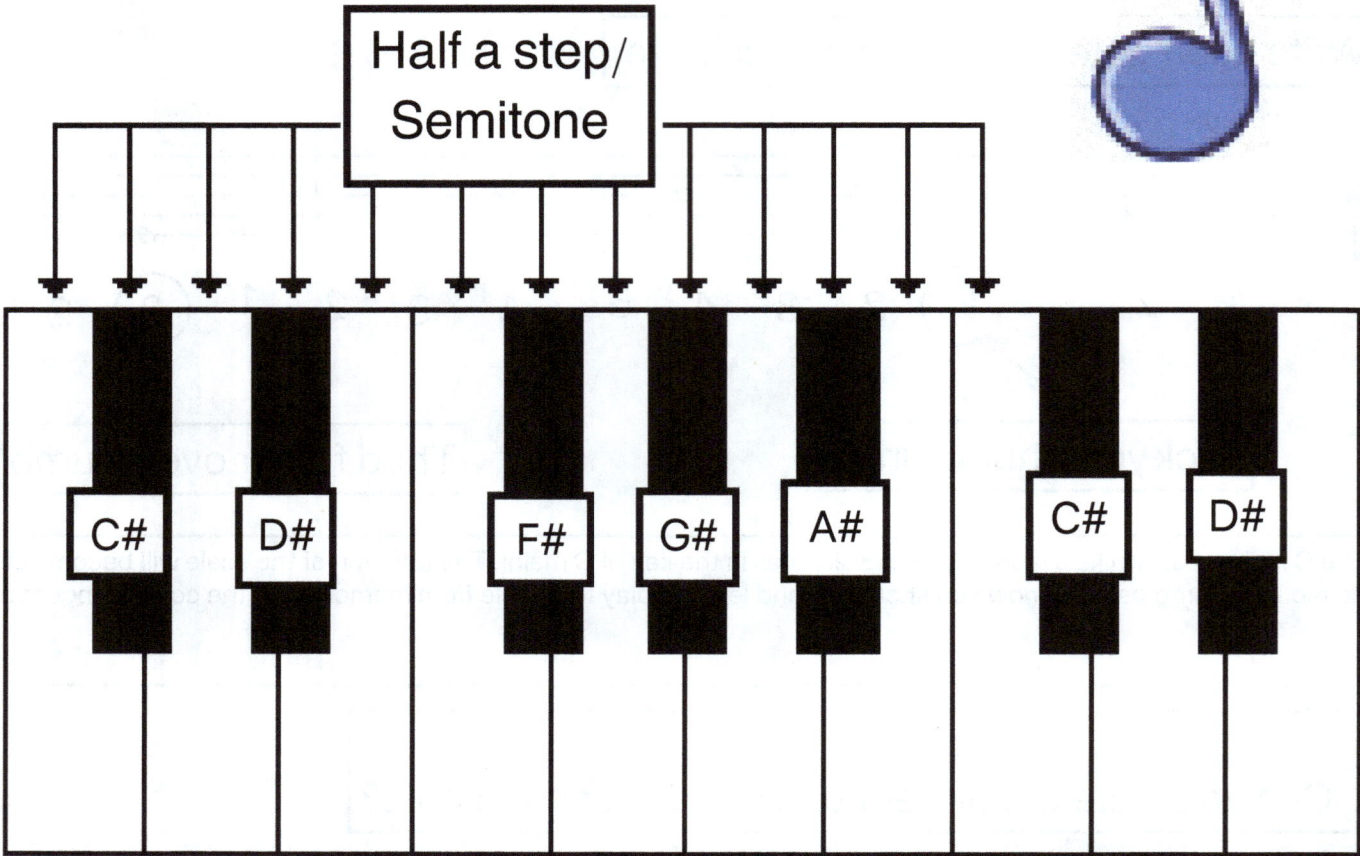

A Sharp is usually the Black key Half a step (semitone) higher than the white key.

A sharp can also be a white key: B# & E#

Mi Guitarra

Style: SwingWaltz
Voice: Guitar

♩=130

In A major

A major pentascale:

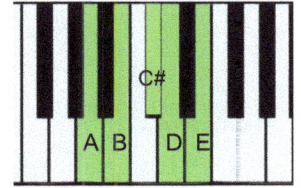

Remains C# for the whole bar

Still C#

Have a look on page 123 to learn the
A major 5 finger scale.

Teacher duet

♩=90

ACMP ON

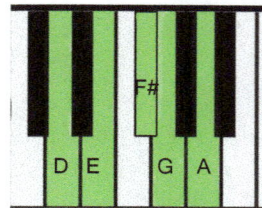

The G Major 5 Finger Scale

G A B C D

This is the G 5 finger scale, also known as a **Pentascale:**
(Pent - means 5 in Greek)

Write the name of the notes below the stave.

Even **G**reat **B**eethoven **D**id **F**orget

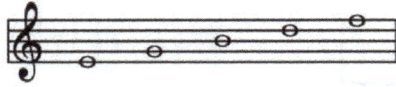

E G B D F

Even Great Beethoven Did Forget

Write the note names under each note.

Can you name the line notes below?

Q. Which note is the highest?

58

Stepping in G

Exercise 2

Style and voice as above

♩ =100

Can you play the Above melody in D Major? Check Page 125
to see the D major5 Finger scale.

Teacher accompaniment for Exercise 1&2

♩ =100   G   D   C   D   G   D   C   G

THE D MAJOR CHORD

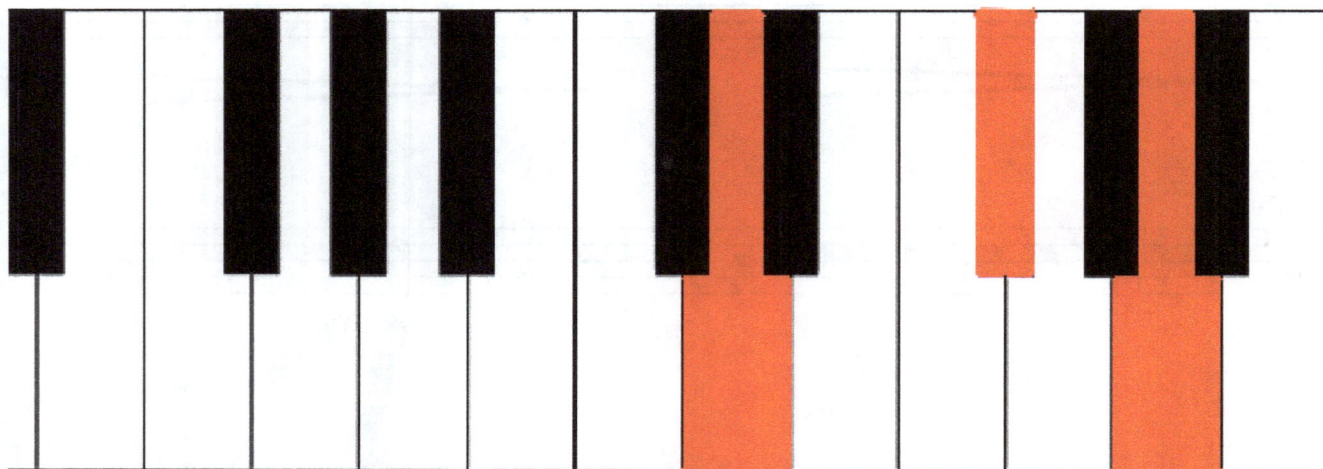

To move between the G chord and the D chord, use a G major inversion.

The G MAJOR INVERSION

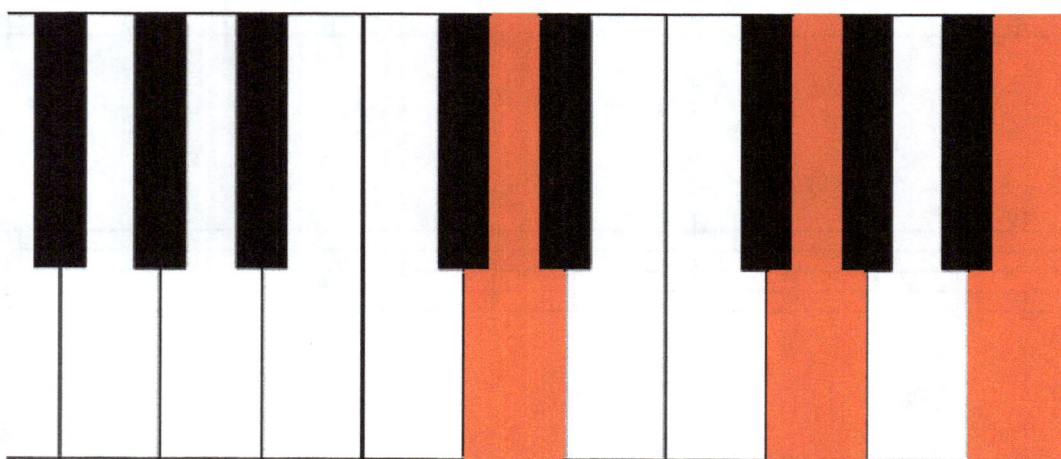

Activity: Practice moving between the two chords with 4 beats on each chord.

Skipping in G major

Style: PolkaPop
Voice: PickBass

♩=130

ACMP ON

Can you play these exercises faster ?

Style and voice as above

♩ = 130

ACMP ON

How many Bs are there all together?
How many Ds are there all together?

Teacher duet for exercise 1&2

ACMP ON

♩=100

61

Euro Trance

Voice: TenorSax
Style: EuTrance
♩=138

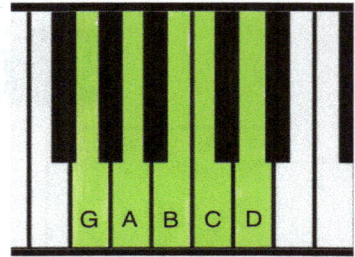

Music Quiz

1. How Many Bs are there?

2. How many times is bar 1 played?

3. How many times does the rhythm in bar 3 play?

4. Can you improvise your own Melody to the chord pattern?

E Minor Chord

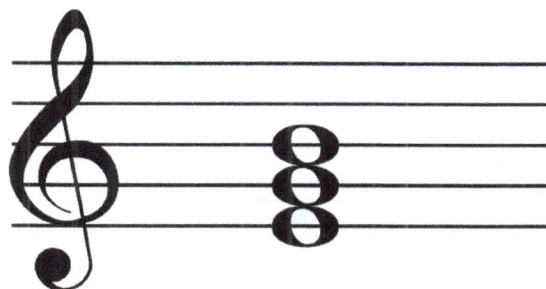

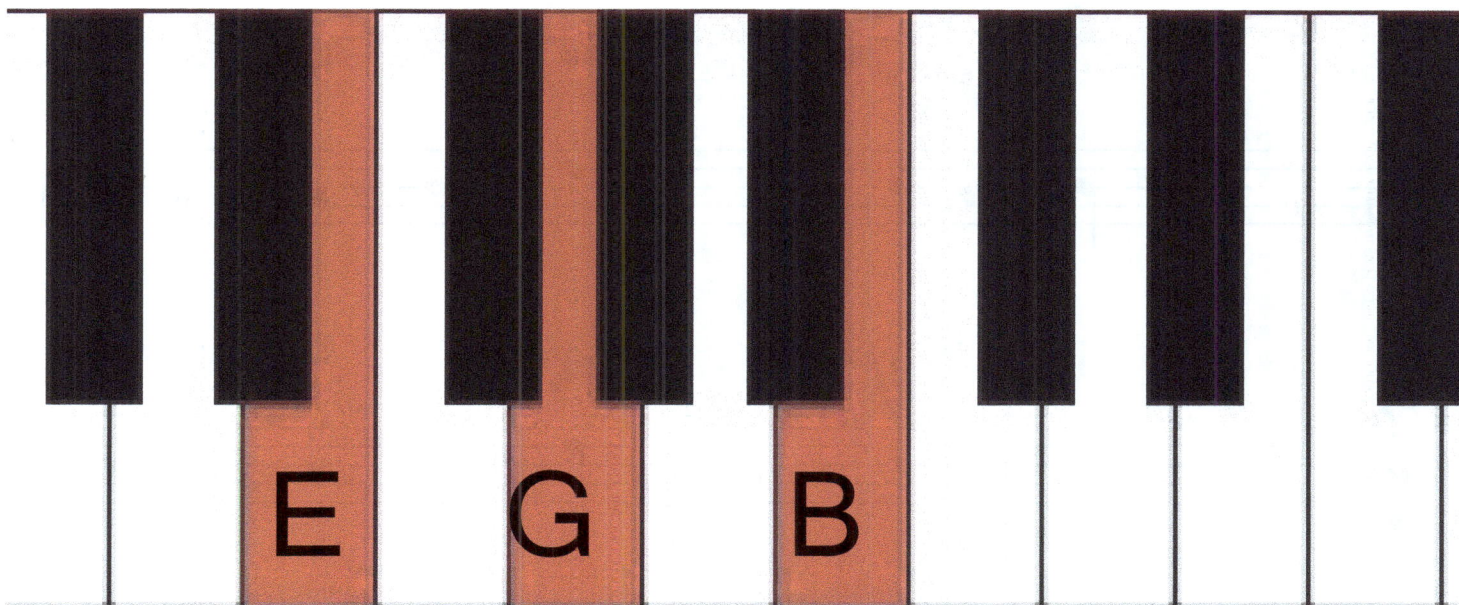

The G Harmony

Style: 8BtAdria

♩=110

MINI QUIZ PAGE

G A B C D

[Musical staff - Line 1]
G — 1 — Em — 2 — C — 3 — D — 4

[Musical staff - Line 2]
G — 5 — Em — 6 — C — 7 — D — 8

[Musical staff - Line 3]
G — 9 — Em — 10 — C — 11 — D — 12

[Musical staff - Line 4]
G — 13 — Em — 14 — C — 15 — D — 16

[Musical staff - Line 5]
G — 17 — Em — 18 — C — 19 — D — 20 — G — 21

1. Circle all the Bs in this piece.
2. How many times in Bar 1 played?
3. How many As are there in this piece?
4. How many times is the chord pattern played?
5. How many Minims are in this piece?
6. Can you play this melody in A major?

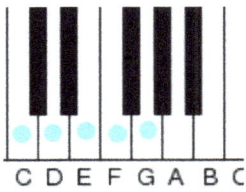

Ode to joy in C major

Ode to joy in G major

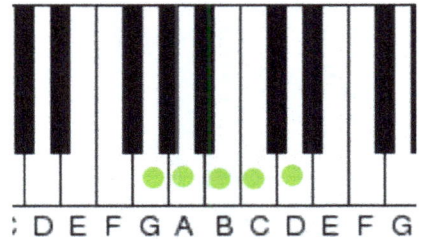

Ode to joy has been transposed to G major. The melody starts on the 3rd note of the scale and follows exactly the same pattern.

Aural Activity : Can you transpose this melody to D major?

65

French Waltz

In G Major

Style: Waltz

♩ = 140

Teacher Duet

♩ = 140

Can you play this melody in C major?

Improvising in G

Style: LoveSong

Activity 1: Students Improvises the rest of the melody.

Activity 2: Students try and play their improvisation with the chords.

Activity 3: Students record their final composition.

RESTS

= 1 beat
Crotchet Rest

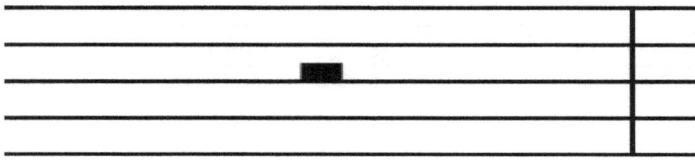

= 2 beats
Minim Rest

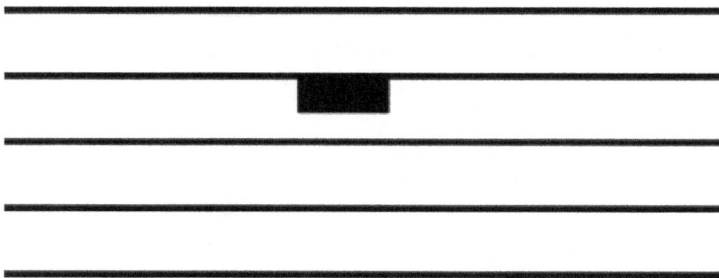

= 4
Beats
Semibreve Rest

Take A Rest

What key is this piece in?

Styles: 16Beat
Voice: Piano

♩=100

ACMF ON

The E major Chord

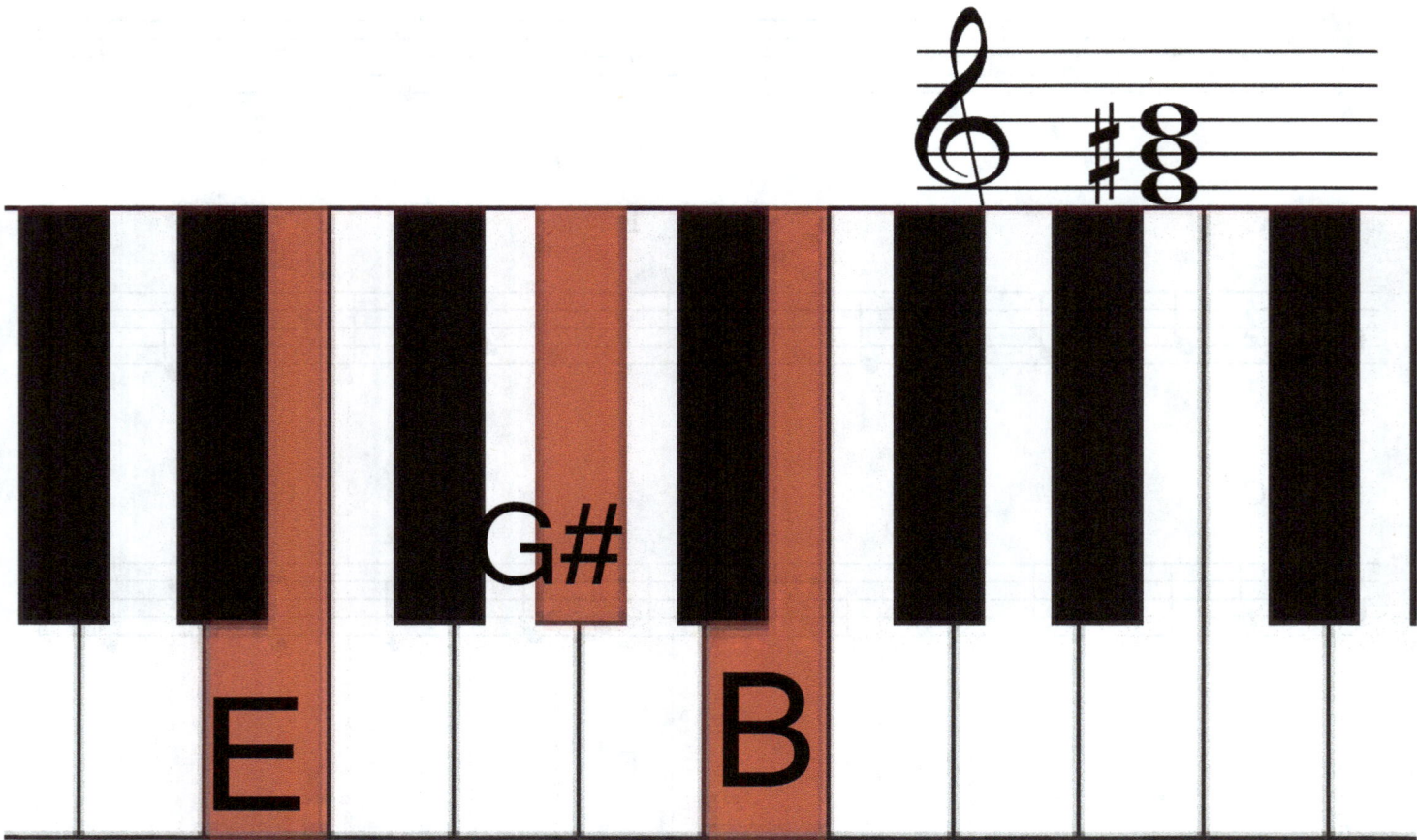

Activity :

Can you try theses chord patterns:

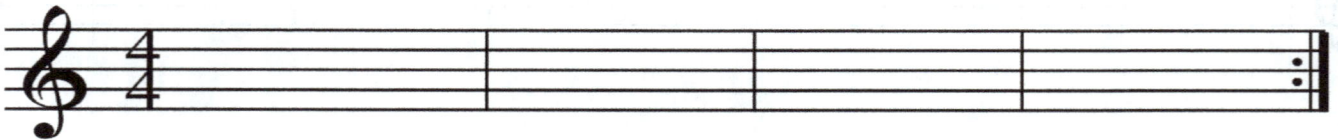

The Spanish Song

In C major/A minor

Style: Swing
Voice: Guitar

♩=150

The Spanish Melody

Style:_____

Voice: _____

♩=130

Fine

Play a B - One step below Middle C - Play

The Spanish Melody

F   21   22   **E**   23   24

Am   25   26   **G**   27   28

F   29   30   **E**   31   32

D.C. al fine

CREATIVE ACTIVITY:

1. Create your own melody using the chords from the Spanish songs. Your melody can use the C 5 Finger Scale and the A minor 5 finger scale.

Teacher Piano duet *Play on separate keyboard/piano.*

$\quarternote = 130$

Fine

D.C. al fine

♭ Flats

Half a step/ Semitone

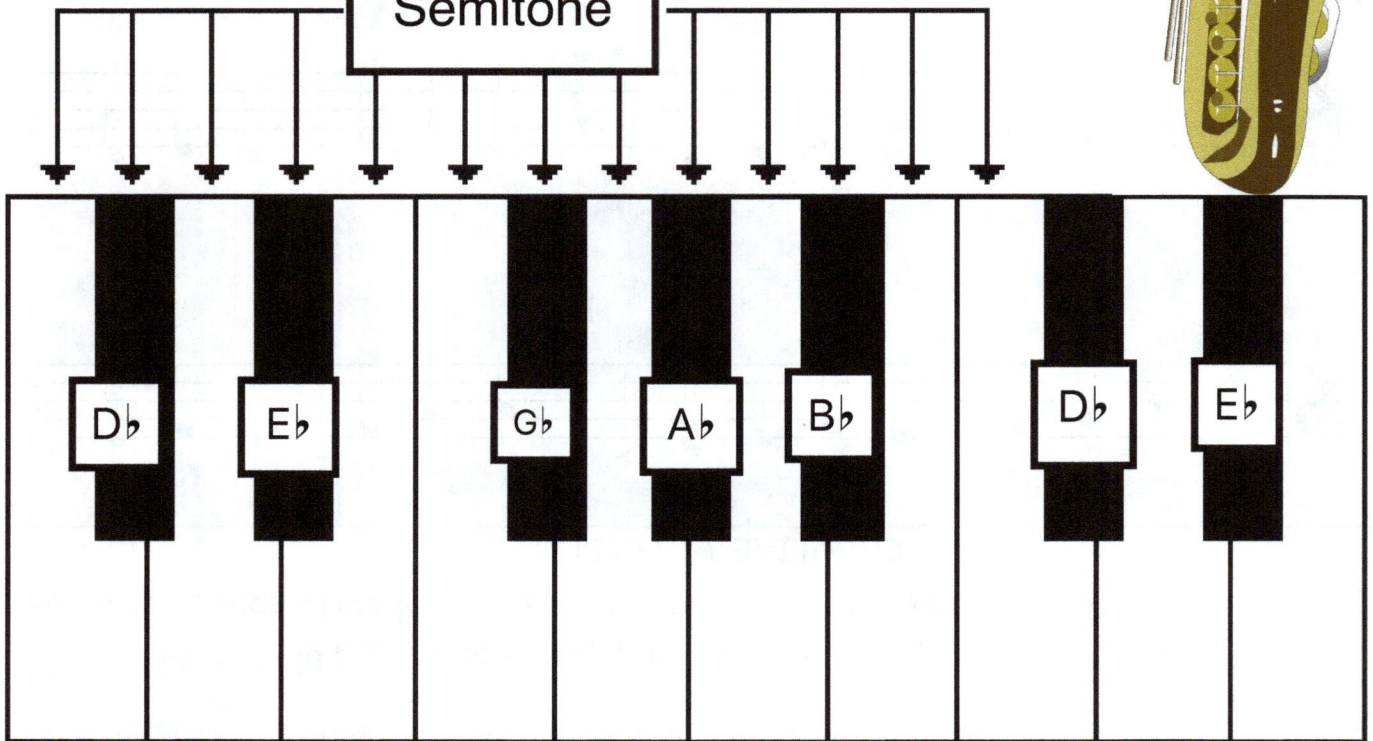

| D♭ | E♭ | | G♭ | A♭ | B♭ | | D♭ | E♭ |

A Flat is the key half a step (semitone) lower than the key before it.

A flat can also be a white key: like C♭ is the same as B
And F♭ is the same as E.

Activity:
Can you find these- B♭,
A♭, E♭, D♭ and F♭?

The Flat Dance

Style:: JazzClub
Voice: Saxophone

♩=120

Teacher Duet

ACMP ON

♩=120

Flat Study

Style: Tijuana/Latin
Voice: Oboe

♩=115

Flat Study 2

Style and Voice as above

♩=100

ACMP ON

Teacher Duets

ACMP ON

♩=115

♩=100

76

F Major Scale

F   G   A   B♭   C

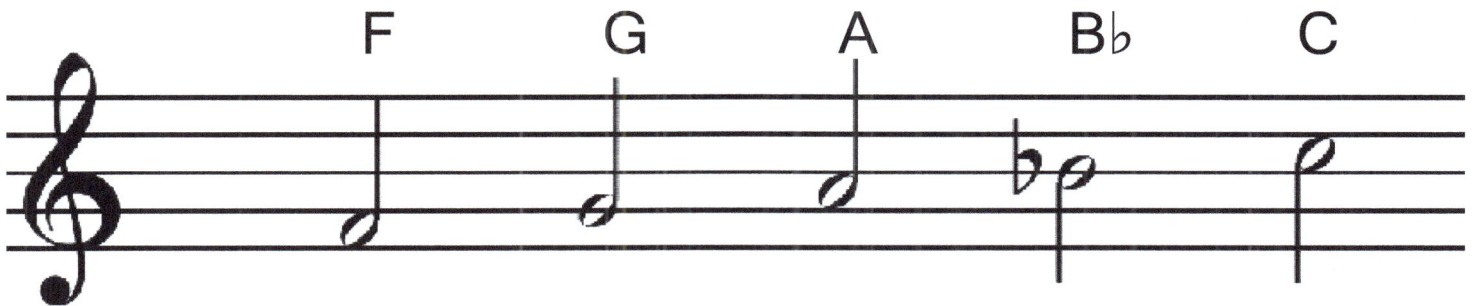

1st 2nd 3rd 4th 5th

This is the F major Pentascale- 5 finger scale

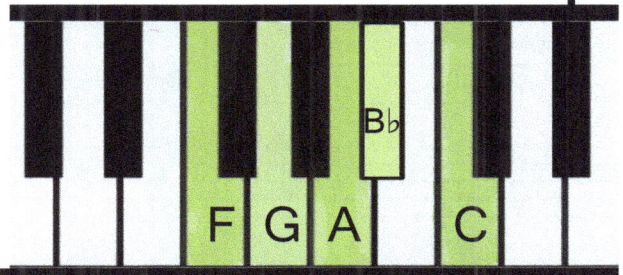

B♭

F G A   C

THE D MINOR CHORD

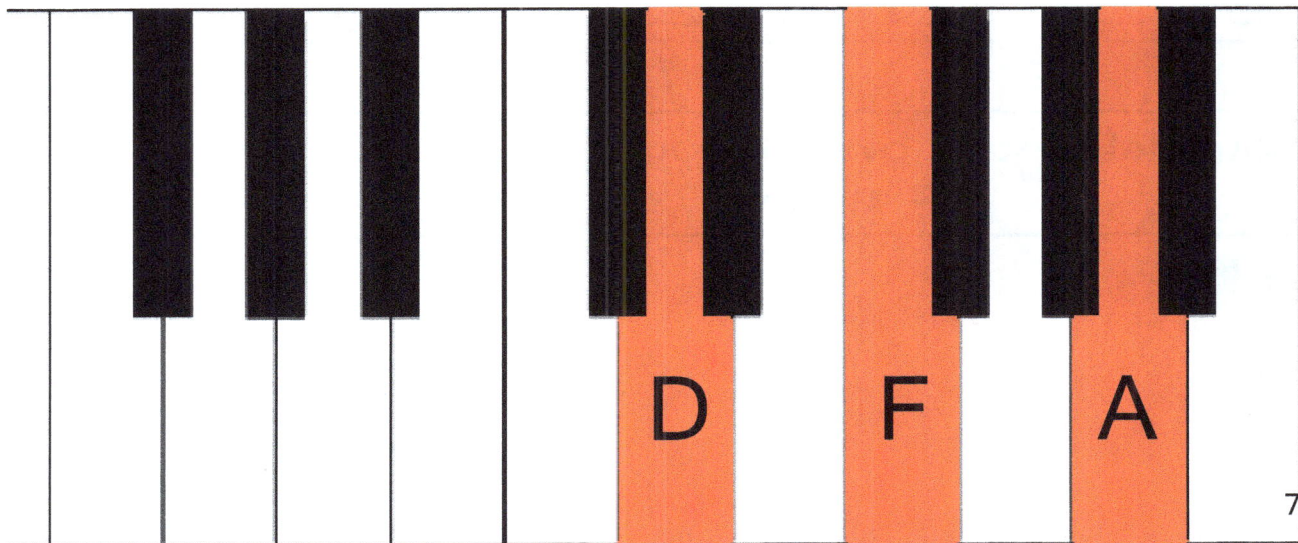

D   F   A

77

Skipping in F Major

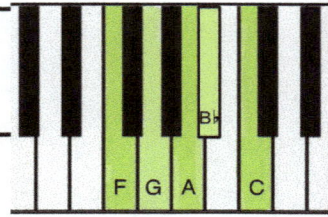

Style: 8Beat
Voice: JazzGuitar

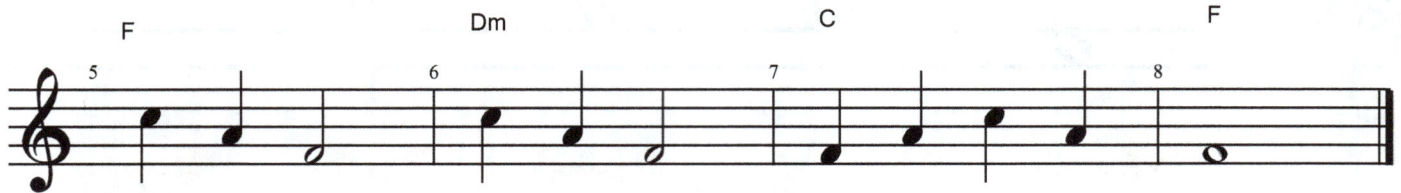

♩ = 116

Exercise 2

♩ = 116 | Style and voice as above |

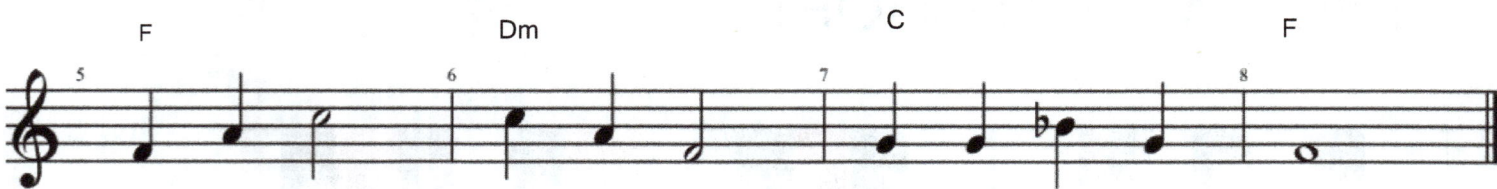

Can you make your own melody using skips in F Major?

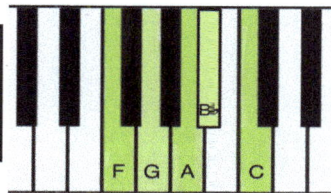

Stepping in F Major

Style: Latin/Samba
Voice: E.Piano

♩=100

Exercise 2

High F 5 Finger Scale

F G A Bb C

Sweet Echos

Style: PopBallard
Voice:Guitar

In F
Major

F major key signature - This shows all the Bs are flats.

Playing in the Key of C Major

The Chords of C Major

Each scale has 7 chords each built on the notes of the scale.

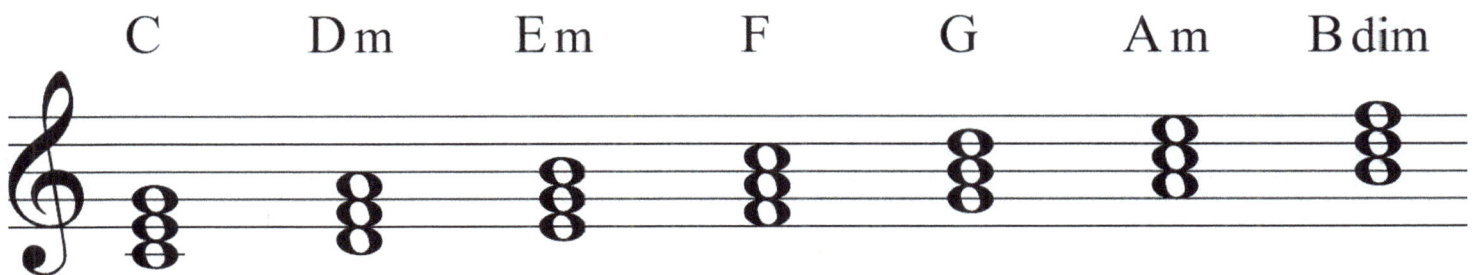

| C | Dm | Em | F | G | Am | Bdim |

Play each chord of the C major scale

You can harmonize any piece in C major with these chords.

The 4th and 5th chord are the most commonly used chords

Broken Chord Ballard

Style: GuitarPop
Voice: Guitar

♩=130

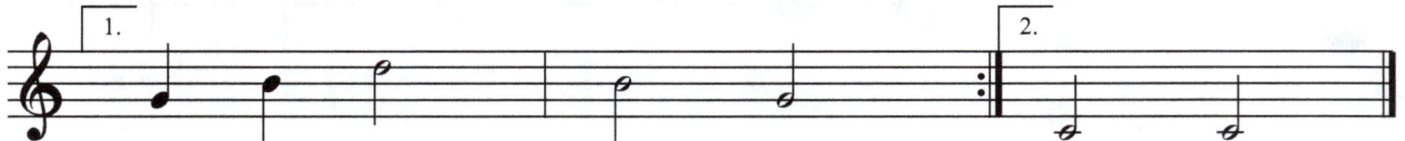

Broken Chords

Broken chords are another way of playing chords. You can choose to play your left hand chords broken, if it adds variety to the song.

1. Can you play this piece playing broken chords in the left hand ? Tip: the hand will play the same notes at the same time.

2. Can you play 'The Easy Tune 1 & 2' with broken chords?

Broken Chord Study

Style: 8BtAdria
Voice: Guitar

♩=100

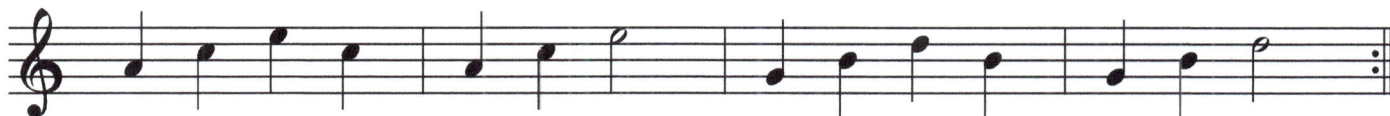

1. Try and play the left hand as broken chords along with the right hand.

2. Can you compose your own lyrics to sing along with the chords?

3. Can you try to change the chord pattern?

Canon in C

Style: Arpeggio

♩=120

Canon In C

1. *Can you create your own melody with the chords?*

2. *Can you play bar 1 - 8 with broken left hand chords?*

Scales

Style: SlowFox

Scales are a very important part of music because each scale is a template on which all melodies are built on. You have learnt the 5 finger scales, now you need to know the full 8 note scales with the correct finger pattern by memory.

G Major

Key Signature: The sharp on F line - Makes all Fs sharp in the music

1 2 3 1 2 3 4 5 4 3 2 1 3 2 1

F Major

The Flat is on the B Line - This Showsall the Bs are Flats

1 2 3 1 2 3 4 5

A Minor

Minors don't have key signatures in there own right

1 2 3 4 1 2 3 4

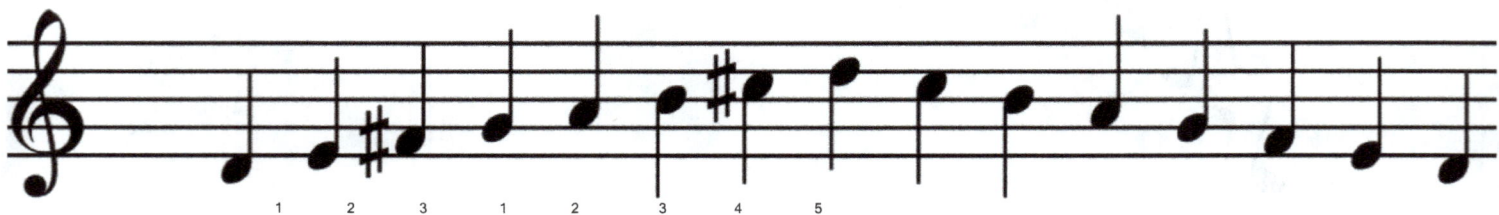

Can you play each scale with the chord in the left hand?

D Major

1 2 3 1 2 3 4 5

Quavers

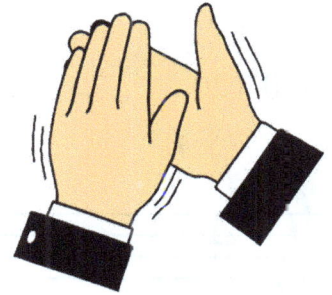

♪ = 1/2 a beat

♫ = Two quavers beamed together.

Rhythm Practice:

4/4   1   2   3   4 | 1 & 2 & 3 & 4 &

4/4   1   2 & 3   4 | 1   2 & 3 & 4 | 1 & 2   3   4

You can also count rhythms using Coffee and tea.

Cof-fee   Tea

Activity: Try tapping this rhythm to a keyboard beat.

Easy Quavers

In C major

Style: Tijuana

♩=90-120

Quaver C Scale

Style: HHLight/Ballard

♩=90

Activity 1 : Improvise a melody using the C 5 finger scale using the above chords.

Activity 2: Now try and improvise using all 7 notes of C scale.

Bonus: Write your creation down on manuscript paper.

Reggae Sundown

Can you clap the rhythm
before you play?

Style: Reggae

♩ = 100

Au Claire De La Lune

French Folk Song

In C Major

Style: Pop

♩=80

Activity: Add the missing boxes correct chords to each box.

Cocktail Jam

Style: HipHop

In A Minor

Try and tap the rhythm before you play

Scherzo

Anton Diabeli

Style: PianoWaltz

♩=150

Scherzo

Minuet In C

Bach
Arranged

Style:
Swingwaltz
♩=120

Can you find the missing chords ?
There are:
2- F chords
2- C chords
2- G chords

Pentascales

C Major
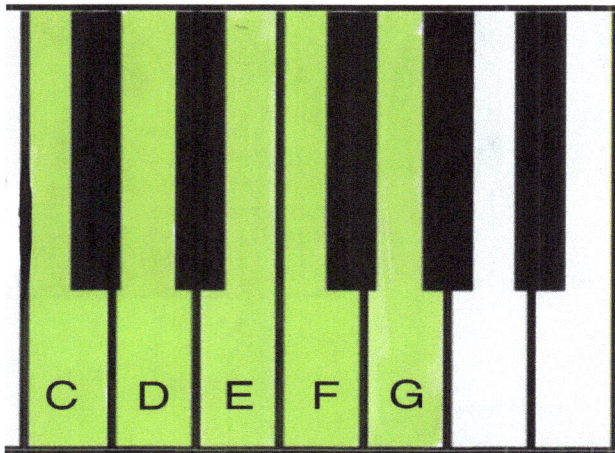
C D E F G

G Major
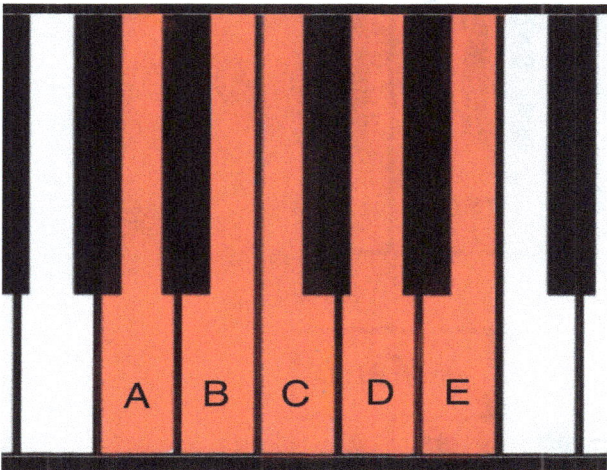
G A B C D

A Minor
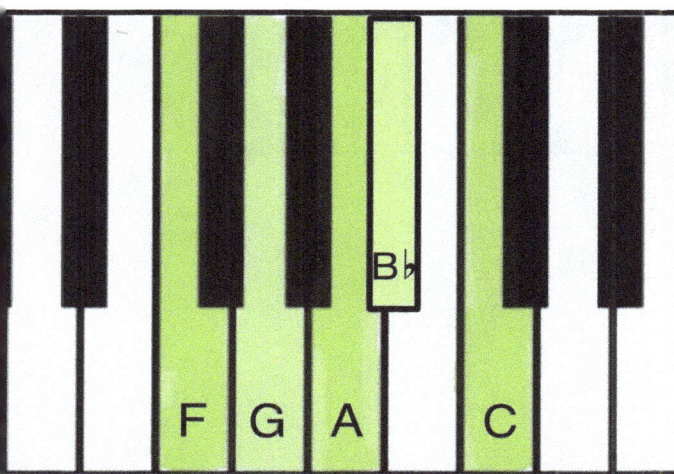
A B C D E

D Major

D E F# G A

F Major
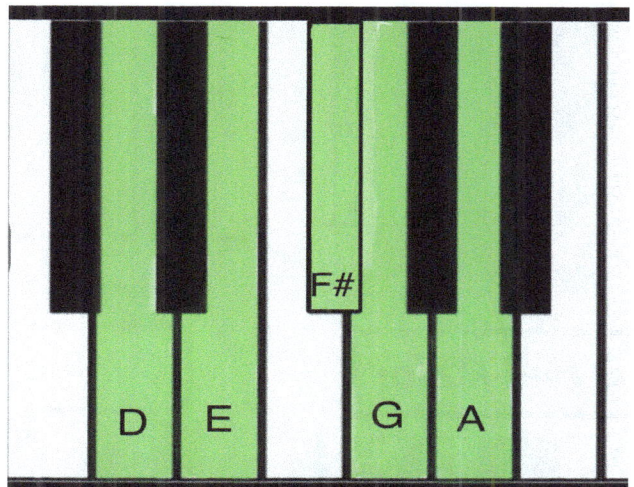
F G A Bb C

A Major
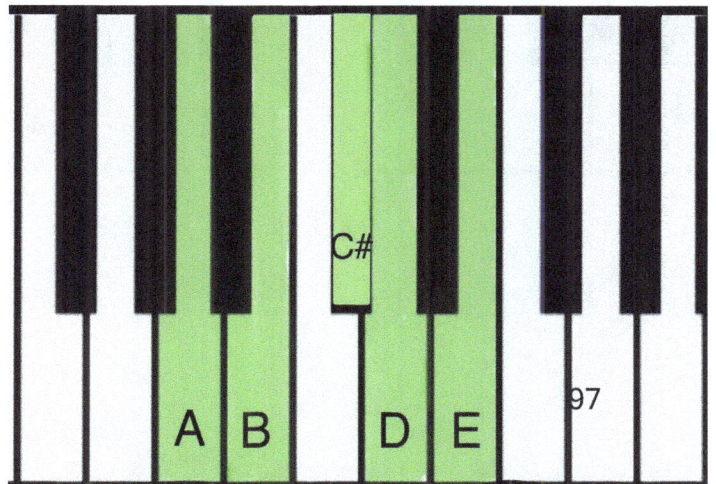
A B C# D E

97

Key Chords

C Major

C E G

G Major

G B D

F Major

F A C

A Minor

A C E

D Major

D F# A

E Minor

E G B

D Minor

D F A

B Flat Major

B♭ D F

C Minor

C E♭ G

A Major

A C# E

Music Achievement

Award

To Certified that _____

Has Completed Acti-learning Keyboard Book 1

Signed _____

Date _____